YOUR TIME IS NOW!

CORPORATE AMERICA TO ENTREPRENEUR

MACK ARTHUR PARKS JR.

Our Time Is Now Publications

Your Time Is Now
Copyright © by Mack A. Parks Jr.
Cover designed by Adrian Meadow, Spartanburg, SC
www.ameadows.me

Published by: Our Time Is Now Publications

For more information, please contact:

Our Time Is Now Publications
PO Box 725211
Atlanta, GA 31139
www.ourtimeisnow.biz

Printed in the United States of America

Your Time Is Now

Mack A. Parks Jr.

ISBN 13: 978-0615877877

Disclaimer: This program is designed for entrepreneurs who will be making $250,000 or less. This book is part of a series. I was encouraged to write the program in small steps so that the reader can track his or her progress. Remaining chapters will be in the next edition.

Table of Contents

Dedication

I would like to thank God first because despite my imperfections, He still shines light on me so that I may see my goals. I would like to thank my parents, Lillie and Mack Parks Sr. of Flint, MI, for their solid support over the years. In whatever business venture I decided to enter, not once have you doubted what I can do. I will always love you for that. As you can see, I am still hard at work. I will never give up.

I would also like to thank my brother Quenton Parks for working with me on this project. I really needed someone to bounce ideas off and help me find those "phrases" that people can relate. Thank you to my sister Angela Gillen and Reginald Parks for their efforts of helping me succeed in my prior business enterprises. We are finally coming out of the woodwork to see the quality of life that we have been seeking. Stay with me; it is time for some fun. I love all of you.

To my ex-wife, Lori Parks Barfield, I am in your debt. You and I have worked on many projects together over the years, and your input has served me well. I will never forget the endless weekends working on the "Grabby Cup" or "Choozey Listener." That was real-time experience. I will always love you for that. To my stepdaughter Bianca, I wanted to let you in on this project around the time of your birthday, but I decided to show you better than I can tell you. I know you did not see this coming, and neither did I. However, I knew something was waiting for me greater than what I could see.

I see a potential in you that is greater than what you see. You have overcome some obstacles that you thought were too high, but now you are attending college. When you take an exam, you always think that you did badly, but you always score 92 or better.

I found out what the problem may be and I hope that this book serves its purpose for you and many others. *You must raise your belief system!* Your homework serves its purpose. Believe it because you earned it! Never let your minimum become your maximum. Love you.

Very special thanks to my friend Keith Holloway. Kitchen table talk really does make a difference! Let us talk more at the table and work through more ideas.

To my friends who are waiting in the wings, Patrick Bailey of Shreveport, La., Chief Technology Officer at Instant Notification LLC, and Peter Lin of Acworth, GA, Chief Engineer at Instant Notification LLC. You guys are worth your weight in gold. I cannot wait for the world to see how talented you guys are.

Mack A. Parks Jr.

Introduction

I am a firm believer that I am not the only one who has a passion for success. I absolutely adore it! However, what most of us have in common is we do not know how to get there. It is so frustrating knowing that your product has great value to the marketplace, but you do not have the skill set or the expertise to make it a reality. A catchy name or a creative marketing scheme is all you have in your vision. You firmly believe that your ideas will work and so do I. This is the reason why we seek help. When you take it as far as you can go, it is time to turn to a professional. I am the guy next door who never gave up on his dreams. I found success because success was looking for me. Now I want to share it with you. From this day forward, you will not second-guess yourself about what you are embarking on or stand still and watch opportunities pass you. Those wonderful ideas that you have been thinking about for so long are about to become a reality. This book is one of the smartest investments that you have made this year. Congratulations!

The focal point of "Your Time Is Now" is for you to follow the seven steps that are laid out in the chapters of this book and write a paragraph under each one so that you can clearly see what you are trying to accomplish. A lot of detailed information lies within your mind because you are constantly thinking about it. Although it may be easy for you to remember in silence about what you are doing, it gets very difficult trying to recite it during a conversation. You do not want to talk too much and lose people's attention. Sometimes when we speak, we may get too lofty and lose sight on what the conversation was all about; you want to stay sharp and precise. Therefore, you should always write your thoughts on paper so that you can keep a clear mind and your work can be secure. Details are important but easy to forget. Sometimes we carry around our ideas in our head for so long that we do not leave room for growth. It is a great feeling knowing that all of your energy and the thought process have been preserve in a place where you can reach out and touch at a moment's notice.

The ultimate goal is for you to be able to give an eight- to 10-minute presentation about your business clearly and professionally. The more you understand about your business, the more you will gain confidence in what you are doing. This will enable you to present your ideas to investors, bankers, clients and the marketplace.

Customers are waiting on you! They are waiting to hear what you have to offer. This is going to be so exciting; you are going to be proud of your accomplishments.

Where Have You Been? I've Been Looking For You!

Congratulations on your decision to become an entrepreneur! I know you have contemplated this subject many times before. We all struggle with this inner secret that lives within us for so long that we do not want anyone to know about it until we hit. Some of your ideas may be five, 10 or 15 years old, but that is okay because entrepreneurship has no age limit. With the help of this book, we are going to finish what you started.

You see, I am going to be your support factor on this business journey, the positive force in your mind. I know that when we concentrate and keep our eyes on the prize, nothing can stop us. No longer will we live in the shadows of our dream, living one way and dreaming of another. We must see ourselves in prosperity *before* it happens. We must come to realize that it is just who we are. We must dispel the voices in our head that cry, "Should I try to reach my goals and dreams?" "Should I stay in captivity and work all my life?" "Can I tell my spouse or significant other?" "Will they laugh at me? Do they think I'm smart enough?" "What would they think of my ideas?" "What will my friends say?" and "You know what happened the last time; quit while you're ahead!"

OMG! It is a constant compromise between thinking and breathing. The negativity will not stop! Can anyone else hear me?

Oh yes, I know how you feel, so let me be clear. *I am on your side!* I will *never* give up on you. I believe in you. You are the reason why I wrote this book. So let us repeat these three words together: "Yes I Can. Yes, I Can. *Yes, I can*! My time is now! Amen.

It's Not Over

I would like to take this opportunity for us to get to know one another so we can have the ultimate business conversation, entrepreneur to entrepreneur, and by the end of this book, *you will be* in position to launch your own business. You are only a stone's throw away from realizing your potential.

One of the most important things that we have in common is that *we are not doing what we are destined to do and o*ur *dreams have yet to be.* We are being held captive by fear that we do not even understand. We go to work five days a week, put on a happy face and tell everyone good morning, good afternoon, or good night and then struggle for the rest of the day. Our mind spins out of control thinking about the project that is long overdue. Something always comes up to take our eyes off the ball. Our subconscious mind tells us to get'er done before someone else beats us to it. It will not leave us alone. It continues to nudge us because it is part of who we are. It is like a monkey on our backs.

However, let me tell you something: that passion that burns deep inside of you that will not leave you alone is greater than anything you have ever done before. It is a personal testament letting you know that *it is not over*. You have work to complete. A good job or great career will never match the fire that lies within your belly. "Oh, Lord, have mercy! How can I escape the imprisonment of work in exchange for a lifetime of entrepreneurship?" I can hear your voice deep in your soul crying out, Get me out of here!" Does this sound familiar? Do I have a witness? Take a firm grip of my hand and lets go and make some MONEY!

What is Motivating Me?

Let me ask you a question: Have you ever driven around your neighborhood and saw people making money in your community but does not live within your community? Do you wonder where they come from, where they live or how they got to where they are? What made them open up a business over here? What do they see that you cannot see? Why are they making money and you are not? Are they better than you are? Are they smarter? Hell No! I know there are at least eight people who live in your neighborhood who think just like you. They are thinking the same exact thing. Where are these folks coming from? The only difference between you and them is that they decided to act on their thoughts. They have done what you are going to do. Your first move was an excellent one when you purchased this book. Your next move is to narrow your focus and believe in yourself.

Some of these same questions were putting pressure on me as well. I had no answers for them. All I knew was trial and error; still I had no choice but to act! However, through those trials and errors I have found the answers that were eluding me all this time, and I can assure you that all of them are in this book.

What most people do not understand about you and me is that you cannot teach our mindset, just as if a college professor cannot teach you anything about passion. It is something that drives from within, pushing us towards our goal. Either you have it or you do not. We want to stay around people with like minds so that we can bounce ideas off one another. It helps expand our mindset and helps us be more creative. Don't you like being around people that can see an opportunity before the opportunity presents itself? Isn't that cool? It is that gift of insight that you cannot buy.

I know you have asked yourself *"Why?"* a thousand times about different products and services that are either not marketed correctly or not positioned properly. Why wouldn't they put one of these over here? They can make a lot more money. On the other hand, why did they wait so long to put one over there? They have lost a lot of money. It is as if we can see missed opportunities everywhere. It comes naturally to us; we have been blessed.

One thing we must constantly remind ourselves is the fact that we *will never get rich by working on a job*! I promise you! Another thing is we must follow through on our commitments so that others see our trail.

Have You Seen Anyone Like This?

Let me ask you another question: Have you seen that guy in the black convertible jaguar that walks into Starbucks every morning with blue jeans and flip-flops? I mean its 10 a.m. on a Tuesday! What time does he have to be at work? What does he do for a living? Oh, he must be running late. This is what we say to ourselves when we encounter this scenario because it is hard for us to imagine someone not working, as we know it, but living how he or she wants to live. It is only natural to hate on someone that is doing something different from what we are doing. After all, you are at work waiting on 12 o'clock so you can take a lunch break. This emotion gets the best of you for only 30 seconds because in the back of our mind, you already know that this man does not have a job and not looking for one. No one goes to work in flip-flops. He has set himself up so that working is only an option. Then, all of a sudden, it starts tugging at you again, reminding you that you have to regain your focus and get back on track to achieve your goals and objectives. It will not leave you alone. That beast within you wants to come out. It is your time to shine.

Entrepreneurship was Talking to Me

Throughout my career, I have been blessed to work for the three largest transportation companies in America. With over 18 years in the industry, I have seen many major changes in how we get products to the customer and to business-to-business. It is a constant realignment of systems, services and customers.

As a courier for one of the largest overnight companies, I delivered packages in upscale residential neighborhoods. No matter how many deliveries I had to make, I had to be finished by 10:30 am, I often wondered how in the world are these same people home every single day. It is not as if they were running late for work because they always came to the door in pajamas and flip-flops and not a care in the world! They came to the door politely, signed for the package, gave me a smile and went on about their business, and I would stand there with a smile on my face shaking my head. "It must be nice," I would say to myself. Jealousy started to get the best of me because I had seen this far too long.

Walking away, I would say to myself, "I know some of my business ideas have some merit to them, and I could make a lot of money too! Hell, I want to smile at somebody at 9:30 in the morning! But there I was, ringing door bells, leaving door tags, running wide open with sweat running down my brow, stress level high, disobeying traffic signs, trying to beat the clock, all for $40,000 a year! "This bull s*^t has to stop! I mean it!" I would say as I jumped back into the truck. However, the funny part about this scenario is, I would do the same thing all over again the next day! It was frustrating. I had to make a change. I knew I could not keep it up because my knees were aching, my back was hurting and my conscience would not leave me alone. I was always asking myself, "When will I get out of here?"

More and more I envisioned myself in that same position: pajamas and flip-flops. I began to feel the relaxation and calmness in their eyes when they came to the door. It was like your first day on vacation, and you do not have to be back to work for two weeks. I want that lifestyle for my family and me. However, wait a minute! There is no way that they could be retired, correct? I mean they are the same age as me. They look like they are between 33-45 years old. They are doing something that I want to do: retire early! I wanted to ask them what business they were in because it may have been something I would like to get into.

Then it hit me — *boom* — like Ali hit Frazier! I already have some business ideas. Why am I not pursuing the blessing that I have already been given? Why am I envious of someone else when I can do the same thing? I have to learn what I need to do, let go of my ego, and realize that I can no longer do this on my own. I needed instructions on how to succeed and I got it! I learned quickly that *you could not do something just because someone else is doing it!* It has to be *genuine*. It has to be *you*. You will not last if you are trying to be somebody else. You may like *how* they are doing what they do, but you do not know *what* it took them to get there. Are you with me?

Let us demonstrate with someone that we all know very well — President Barack Obama. Millions of people love him. Some folks hate him. Some folks try to be like him. They try to emulate his presence, his walk, his vernacular, his style of dress, his oration, his stature, and even his swagger. Nevertheless, you cannot get to his level of sophistication by reading a few books or looking at cable television. You have to go through the rigors of local and national debates, community organizing, campaign orchestration, fundraisers, keynote speaking engagements, constituent services, triumphs and the heartache of Capitol Hill. You have to develop tough skin to handle news organizations like CNN, CBS, The New York Times, The Washington Post, and constant interviews with Fox News, MSNBC, ABC and the U.S. House of Representatives. Then when he is done with all that, he still has to go home and tune in to Michelle, Sasha and Malia. You have to go through your own process of rigor in order to achieve your success. People can relate to you when you are honest.

I did not know it at the time, but that last vision I had was the last straw. Entrepreneurship had given me an ultimatum. It said, "Go in the direction that I told you or finish failing!" (Keep working!)

I still did not quite understand because I had gotten comfortable with $40,000 a year. Entrepreneurship had sent me enough signals and too many examples for me not to act. I have learned firsthand that entrepreneurship lives within you, and it only deals with the truth. It is in your walk, your attitude, your conversation and your dress, and it shows on your face. Some folks may call this "swag," but if you are on a job, these characteristics cannot coexist! It is either one or the other.

My manager used to ask me questions about the job, its functions, how it relates to me, and tips on how we can better serve our customers. Then I would answer with a smart-mouth entrepreneurial spirit as if I hired him. He would give me tasks to do, and I would do them as an entrepreneur would. He would warn me from time to time, and I respected it as an entrepreneur would. My actions and thoughts have left the employee mindset. I am going about my job as though I am working for myself. After all, he was not telling me anything that I had not already heard. Nevertheless, that is not the point.

So on June 16, entrepreneurship and my boss must have had an explosive conversation because they came to the same conclusion that I have strayed away into my own understanding, and it was time to set me free. He gave me my marching papers that read "Goodbye! Your services are no longer needed for this company." I was stunned, shocked, confused, excited and free. Then I heard a voice in my head that said, *"Go in the direction that I was telling you to go or finish failing!"*

"Huh? Oh! Oh! That is what you were trying to tell me. I didn't understand you." I had gotten comfortable with $40,000 a year. It was not my true calling. Something else is waiting on me. I always wondered why I was having dreams that I did not have a job to go to when I woke up in the morning. Entrepreneurship was talking to me.

Finally, I can find my purpose. That job and I parted ways. I had enough of it and it had enough of me. There was a mutual understanding, that I was given an opportunity to return to that job, but that second thought kicked in my head that said, *"Risk must be taken."*

I was excited because I knew I had enough saved to live on for 36 months, and it strengthened my courage. Then the other thought kicked in my head: *"Stay on the job and live in captivity."* I became defiant and determined. My emotions were all over the place. I never knew that determination had tears. Fear tried to persuade me by saying, "Entrepreneurship can wait! You got 10 more years before you can retire. What are you going to tell your friends and family? This is a tough economy; jobs are hard to come by these days." Nevertheless, freedom reminded me, "You were ahead of the curve the last time you ventured out, but you didn't stick with it. You watched a $1 billion industry unfold right before your eyes, and you got no part of it. Now here you are again, ahead of a $1 trillion industry. Do you really need to think about this?" I declined the offer because the time had come for me to quit talking about it and make something happen. It was time for me to stop being selfish by keeping my work in my head and putting it in the marketplace where it belonged. I told myself that thousands of customers are waiting on me. I rehearsed it so many times in my mind that I started to believe it. All of a sudden, I felt my "swag" coming on. *"I have to complete my project. I have to secure my future,"* I said to myself. That thought instantly made me free.

There is nothing in the way to stop me from building my bridge to prosperity.

"Sometimes you must experience a loss in order to appreciate a gain."

-Mack A. Parks Jr.

My Time Is Now!

Exxon Mobile profits are up 3 billion in one quarter! Facebook is preparing an IPO valued at $100 billion! The U.S. economy is recovering from a five-year hangover and entrepreneurship has never wavered. Ladies and Gentleman, "This is America, where energy, economies and entrepreneurs meet!" There is no other place on the planet like this. No one has the imagination for innovation, as we do. We truly believe that there is always something new to bring to the table. That is why other countries such as Europe, China, India and Mexico look to us for leadership. They understand that America has mastered the game of capitalism and they want to play.

Wall Street went bankrupt and Leman Brothers went out of business. Gas at the pump is approaching $5 a gallon, and Iran is threatening nuclear war. Osama Bin Laden was killed and the Arab spring has risen. Eighty percent of U.S. homes have lost 50 percent of their value while the federal government capped health care costs. Politicians are playing political football with the debt ceiling, and the world economy is looking for a bailout!

Who in the world would want to start a business in this uncertain economy? The answer is quite simple: you and me. During periods of recession and uncertainty, business models are forced to change. It is time for something new.

Every year in the United States entrepreneurs line up to stake their claim in the global marketplace. At the sound of the bell, they take off running with a burst of energy, armed with fresh ideas, broke, and no clue to where they are going. It is one of the proudest moments of their lives. "Liberty at last" is what they are yelling, but the reality is that it is only the seasoned entrepreneur that makes the headlines. They have been around the block once or twice and paid their dues before someone gave them a break and funded their idea. Nevertheless, I am like you. I do not have time to wait in line and wait for someone to call my name. I might be overlooked. I cannot afford to pay dues by letting opportunities slip away! My time is *now*! I cannot wait any longer!

To all my fellow Americans and aspiring entrepreneurs, your spirit is in the right place, but now it is time to get your mind right and get in the game.

Hello, my name is Mack A. Parks Jr., author of the book "Your Time Is Now!" Let us get started.

The Winner's Circle

I am going to take you on a journey to the beginning of a company that I started 12 years ago and the path that I took to be successful. It is an entrepreneurial story that has ideas, hope, defeat, courage and success. My story may be your story or vise versa, but what is important is that we finish the race because in the end, we win.

The first few steps were very important to me because I had a keen sense of urgency, and I wanted to stay focused so that I could follow the trail to where I was going. However, I will admit that I did some tail chasing and goose hunting, but I was hell bent on putting my product in the marketplace. Now I have grown. I have learned the necessary steps that are required to be in the winner's circle of business.

The winner's circle, now that's a nice cliché isn't it. Nevertheless, we really mean it! None of us wants to put in countless hours of energy, time and money only to come in second place. Second place to us means that we are still on the job. That is okay for most people, but we want to hold up the trophy! We want to stand in the middle of the ring and be declared the winner, by a knock out! I know you cannot wait to show your peers what you have been up to the last couple of years. You told them it was going to work!

I have that same fire that you have. It never leaves me. You know when you are speaking to an entrepreneur because you can speak for hours on subjects that ordinary people cannot comprehend. I knew I was going to be an entrepreneur long before I knew what an entrepreneur was. I have a certain type of hustle in me that is not intended for a job.

Cash is Universal

When I went into the military at age 19, I used that time to find my way through life and learn some skills that would be valuable to me later on. One of the skills I found by accident was the art of communication. I remember being overseas in China, Subic Bay, Philippines and Mombasa, Kenya and bartering was my way to get what I wanted. These places did not have shopping malls, so you had to purchase goods and services from street vendors. There were no price tags. Whatever price the vendor told you was the price you had to decide on — was it worth the investment or not? Therefore, here come the negotiations. I liked the bartering back and forth and then settling on a price that we both could live with. He was trying to get the best of me, and I tried to get the best of him. I was surprised at how good I was because other people started coming to me so that I could negotiate for them to get what they wanted. Nevertheless, the real skill set was this: *I do not* speak Chinese, Swahili or Filipino. What I understood was value and cash! Once they understood where I was coming from, they asked me very nicely to step aside while they conducted their business and they would give me what I wanted later. In other words, I was interfering with their profits. Now keep in mind that none of these merchants could speak a lick of English, but I understood them very well. You see, cash speaks all languages. It does not matter what country it came from.

If You Believe it Will Happen, Then it Will Happen

After six years in the military, I started to grow into another way of thinking. My mind started expanding. I learned a few lessons in life that will be with me forever. However, the thought of me wearing dungarees and Dixie cup hats for the next 20 years was not appealing to me. I knew back in high school in Flint, MI, that I wanted to dress nice in whatever occupation I was working in, so I decided to leave the military for civilian life and find my true calling. I worked a few odd jobs in the transportation industry that helped increase my skill set in communications, but nothing prepared me for the exciting times that came to the south in 1992. I was living in Cobb County, GA, when Omar Sharron announced, "…And the winner of the 1996 Summer Olympic Games goes to the city of *Atlan-tah*!" It was as though time stood still for one minute.

No one could believe that a southern state could pull off something that big. Local residents were proud of Atlanta. Everybody's pagers were beeping throughout the day. People were trying to get the details on who, what, when and where. As everyone was still celebrating and congratulating each other, I was standing still in my living room thinking to myself, *"What could I bring to the table that people want to buy?"*

I was working for an asset protection company during the mid 90s. Work was plentiful at that time because the city wanted to show that they had everything under control. Atlanta was in the midst of getting herself ready for the big dance. One day on a hot Friday afternoon, my supervisor posed a question to me that I would never forget. He said, "I have a position opening at one of our biggest accounts in downtown Atlanta; are you interested? I asked, "Which account are you referring to?" He said, "The Atlanta Olympic Committee." I stood there with a grin on my face so big that you would have thought I was the joker from the Batman movie. "This cannot be happening to me," I thought. I reached out quickly to shake his hand and answered with a firm grip to express gratitude.

Have you ever had those moments in life where you said aloud what you wanted and then a couple months later it came to pass? Well I was in that moment. All I could think about was the day I asked myself, "What could I bring to the table that people want to buy?" I got my wish, now I have to produce something. I could imagine some of my friends saying, *"Be careful what you ask for because you just might get it!"* I also remember once hearing a multimillionaire say, *"If you are seeking success, then success is seeking you."* Hot damn! That was the type of energy that I was walking around with!

He must have felt my spirit because my spirit was feeling him.

"Why not go out on a limb? Isn't that where the fruit is?"

—Frank Scully

Atlanta is Ripe for Entrepreneurship

Atlanta became the brightest star in the south during the early 1990s and it remains that way today. Mayor Maynard Jackson was the man in charge at the time and on a mission beaming with pride. You could almost tell that he knew something the world did not. He exuded confidence as he walked the grounds of city hall and Atlanta's favorite hot dog spot called The Varsity. Residents of Atlanta knew something big was about to happen, but they did not know to what extent. You see, Atlanta is rich in history. Some locals can tell you the story of what most people do not see on television or read in textbooks.

There are numerous people still around who recall the Civil Rights Movement with Dr. Martin Luther King. They live in the same houses they lived in when he marched through their neighborhoods. They can also tell you about Ralph David Abernathy, Rev. Joseph Lowery, former Mayor Andrew Young, Hosea Williams and Coretta

Scott King. These are some of the most recognized names on the planet. They represent struggle for change around the world.

I think this is what former Mayor Maynard Jackson was calculating — highlighting Atlanta's history and promoting the future. The Olympic Games would give people a chance to appease their curiosity about the south. However, when they arrived here, there would be more to the story.

Atlanta is a new city! It is the brightest star in the south. Fresh air, warm weather, nice paved roads, higher education, public transit, cheap real estate, low taxes, clean city, modern rail system, strong middle class and an international airport. You can go anywhere in the world from Atlanta. All these attributes translated into big business for the City of Atlanta and the State of Georgia. Major corporations would take a second look at Atlanta when considering relocating their business or building new plants. This city already had infrastructure in place. All you would have to do is plug in.

I believe this is what the mayor knew but the world did not. The residents knew something big was about to happen but not to the magnitude that they see today — CNN, MLB Champions, NFL, TNT,

Tyler Perry Studios, country superstars, R&B superstars, gospel music, mega churches, music capital of the south … and it is still growing!

Dr. King said he had a dream. He also said he had been to the mountaintop. When he looked over, I wonder did he see how beautiful Atlanta is today. Did he see the strong legacy that Mayor Jackson left behind? Did he see the first African-American female mayor of Atlanta, former Mayor Shirley Franklin? Did he see the strong leadership from one of the youngest mayors in America today, Mayor Kaseem Reed? I wonder what else he dreamed about. What's next for the City of Atlanta?

Money, Power, Testosterone and Pretty Women

Downtown Atlanta is nice in the summertime. People are moving at a casual pace and having lunch in the park. The ice cream man is serving popsicles and people are playing chess at the city square. On my arrival to the Atlanta Committee of the Olympic Games, the view was something that I will never forget. The buildings were tall with mirrored windows. Lincolns and limousines lined up outside waiting to pick up clients, flags from over 100 countries were hung from the top of the ceilings, and floors were buffed and polished to resemble glass. The place just smelled like money. The men were dressed to the nine's. Even the mailroom clerks were neat. Brooks' Brothers suits, Johnston Murphy shoes, custom ties, bright cuff links, crisp white shirts and Kenneth Cole brief cases. As for the women, OMG! They were just as beautiful as they were professional. Two-piece skirts just above the knee with splits on the side, 2-inch heels on earth toned shoes, fresh paint on the fingernails and toes, Victoria Secret perfumes, Toni Braxton hairdo's, all with an attitude that screamed, "I am blessed and highly favored." Sometimes it was hard to tell if I was in church or at the BET Awards. I just knew I was in the right place at the right time.

After I adjusted to the scenery, I regained my focus. I thought about the question I asked myself when the games were first announced, and during the jubilation that followed: "What could I bring to the table that people want to buy?"

I'm About to be a Millionaire!

My skill set was in communications, so I wanted to be in a position of persuasion. A couple of months on the job went by before something piqued my interest. The one thing I noticed most was when employees started traveling on the road they always wanted some riding music so they would not get bored while going through small towns. They were constantly looking for real estate to host an Olympic competition around the southeast. Downtown Atlanta could not support all the Olympic events.

I suggested to one of the women to flip through the channels and listen to the radio, but they wanted more than that. They wanted to keep the same type of music from city to city. That was hard to do. I did not understand what the big deal was until I started traveling on the road myself. I found out that good radio stations were rare, especially if you only wanted to listen to one genre. Not only did you have to constantly search for good music every time you went through a city, but you also had to remember the station the radio was playing when it was time to go back.

This became nerve racking and frustrating because I could not remember exactly where I was when I picked up a radio station. It got to a point where I found myself writing down radio stations and the city they were in versus trying to remember them in my head. This method paid off and made my trip a lot more relaxing. Now all of a sudden I did not mind traveling long distances anymore. My frustrations were minimized. I began to understand the saying, "Necessity is the mother of invention."

Less than five minutes after that thought, a green light popped in my head. At this moment, I knew that I was blessed by God and led by faith. It was my action of looking for a solution that led me to the light. I thought, "If writing down the radio stations did wonders for me, will it do the same thing for people who are looking for pop, country, rock, band, news talk or soul music? The thump of excitement in my heart told me, *"Yes!"* I had discovered something that no one else was doing, and I did not need a second opinion. My confidence had confirmed that there was no need for research. Just make it happen! I was all in. I am about to be a millionaire!

When I got back to the job, I looked at all those people who had asked for riding music as potential customers. No way was I going to tell them about my new discovery. I went to work on it right away. I could not waste any time. The Olympics would be here shortly and I wanted to have something to sell. I figured that I would take my product and put it in all the welcome centers across the Southeast United States — Georgia, Florida, Alabama, Tennessee, Mississippi, Louisiana, South Carolina and North Carolina. I was feeling it!

My work shift was from 3 p.m. to 11 p.m., Monday – Friday. I had at least 4 hours a day to work on my project before I went to work. I remember the first time I went to the local library. I asked the clerk, "How can I look up radio stations that are located in the southeast United States?" She came from behind the counter and guided me to the section that I asked for. The area looked intimidating. The books were so large and thick; I thought I was at the law library of congress. I was hesitant to open one because I thought I might find the case of Roe vs. Wade.

As I starting looking into the books, there were volumes of information that I was not aware of; it gave me demographics of cities and towns that sparked my interest. I could not believe what I found. I could make a ton of money with all this information. The library has a wealth of data! I see why all those people were selling books about how to get a government grant and how to buy a home with no money down! It is all in the library free! Nevertheless, I was not interested in that. I just wanted radio station information.

"Leadership is about action, not position."

—Cynthia Parks

People Don't Buy What You Like!

As I sat down and started gathering my information, I noticed there were different ways of putting my program together. I could do it electronically or in print. I chose print because it was easier to complete and the cost was low. Picking out radio stations and formats was exciting to me. Finally, I am in charge of what consumers can listen to and I absolutely did not ask anyone a question about what I was doing. I said to myself, "I got this!"

I like music from the 70s because I think it carries a lot of weight. Some music that we hear today is a reflection of that. I also believe that it has held its value throughout the years. As a kid, you really did not know the meaning of the lyrics that was often played on the radio. You just know that it sounds good and everybody likes it. As you mature into an adult, those same songs have a total different twist. You begin to understand the lyrics and the message in the song. Music today is all about the commercial appeal, record spins, controversy and who got shot. Can you imagine that being shot gives you street credibility? It is sad but true. Local DJs used to have a pulse on the community. They knew what would move people. When they put on music like "What's Going On?" by Marvin Gaye, listeners felt where the DJ was coming from, and late at night a DJ would play music that made you want to get married, stay together or say hello three times. "I Heard It through The Grapevine," meant that you said something disrespectful or inappropriate and it got back to you. Music was the art of expressing our feelings to one another. "Sara Smile" by Hall and Oats was a song that made a man feels good when a woman gave a friendly gesture. This is how we dealt with issues. The artist had tuned into the people and got the pulse of the city. Little did we know that songs from our childhood past would be classics today? In my opinion, the 70s music helped us fall in love with the art of communication. Where is that today? All I hear about is that thin piece of paper that carries a lot of weight. Now who sang that song?

I concentrated on music that my close circles of friends liked and what I liked. Before I knew it, my program started looking like the music chart in jet magazine. I knew half of them would not buy my program; they would want it free or half price. I valued their opinion. Looking at my program again, I noticed that I did not have much of any other genre listed. Then something hit me — *boom*! — like Marvin Haggler hit Tommy Hearns. My revelation was, *"People don't buy what I like, but they buy what they like."* So why was I putting so much energy into making a program specifically for me when I was not the one who was buying it? It was time to wake up and smell the coffee because not everyone likes what I like.

This revelation hit me so fast I felt like I was broke before I got started. "Your friends will not make you rich," I told myself. Actually, I decided not to tell them anything until I was finished. I had to back track and refocus. I could not afford to let my emotions of the past hold me back from the future of tomorrow. Times had changed, and this was business. I had to give the people what they wanted!

For the next seven months, I spent most of my time at the library until I completed my mission. Sometimes work can be fun! Never in my life have I concentrated that much to complete a task. I had every major radio station in the southeastern United States listed in my book. I made sure I had music from all genres, including news talk and big band. I was so proud of myself that I smelled freedom around the corner. It reminded me of my last day of school when I knew I did not have to go back. "*I am done*! I am about to retire. I'm about to show all my friends and coworkers that I had it in me all the time." No longer would I *talk* about being rich, I was *going to be* rich!

I worked so long and hard on my book that I never realized I did not have a title for it. I thought of all kinds of corny names like "Highway Radio Guide," "Radio Traveler," "I Got the Music," etc. Then all of a sudden, one of my favorite songs "Choosy Lover" by The Isley Brothers played on the radio. That song hit the nail right on the head. The title of my book would be, "Choozey Listener Radio Travel Guide." I fell in love with that title. I felt that I was giving people a choice of what they wanted to listen to while driving on the road.

Just Winging It

Once I gathered my information, I started looking for a graphic artist and a data entry person to complete my book. It did not dawn on me that I was an entrepreneur until I started asking for help. I thought everyone would feel my excitement and work with me free until we made a profit. Uh-uh, it did not work like that. I had to barter my way through this. I did whatever I had to do to get what I needed; I left no stone unturned. Whatever they wanted or needed, I went and got it. My associates were computer geeks. All they wanted was $500 software by Apple and Microsoft. This was right up my alley because "I have a certain type of hustle in me that was not intended for a job."

I made a few phone calls and a few promises, and I got both packages for $375. I thought, "All I had to spend was under $400 to complete a book? I'm going to be rich for real!"

While my newly found associates were doing their work, I contacted Georgia's Department of Industry, Trade & Tourism for an appointment. I wanted to make sure that I got "Choozey Listener" into all welcome centers in Georgia. I am thinking big! After I started dialing, I started thinking about contacting AAA Motor Club, local car dealerships, truck stops and convenient stores as well. My mind was spinning into riches. With just one phone call, all these other options popped in my head. This is what happens when you start working on your action plan.

I wrote a letter to the Georgia Department of Industry, Trade and Tourism. I have included a copy here:

October 2, 1995

Ms. Hanna Medford, Deputy Commissioner

Georgia Department of Industry, Trade and Tourism

285 Peachtree Center Avenue, NE

Marriott Marquis Two Tower, Suite 1000

Atlanta, GA 30303

Dear Ms. Ledford:

My name is Mack A. Parks Jr., owner of Max Multi Media, Inc. I am a small business entrepreneur based in Smyrna, GA, who read your article in the Atlanta Journal Constitution regarding support of the man who wants to sell T-shirts through vending machines at State Welcome Centers. I think that is a terrific idea. However, there is another product I would like to introduce to the travel industry that will benefit Southeastern travelers and the Georgia Department of Industry, Trade and Tourism both economically and informatively. My thought was that the product would serve 11 Southeastern states and would do well in the Welcome Centers. The publication was called the "Choozey Listener Radio Travel Guide."

This guide was design to assist vacationers, business and leisure travelers as to what types of stations are on the radio as they travel from city to city throughout the Southeast. The "Choozey Listener" had all of the radio music formats covering every age group from Adult Contemporary, Album-Oriented Rock, Hot Country, Christian Radio, Oldies, Urban Contemporary, Easy Listening, News, Weather, Pop, Rock, and Top 40. As well as syndicated radio, talk show hosts like Sean Hanitty, Steve Harvey, Tom Joyner, Rush Limbaugh, Al Sharpton and Howard Stern all formatted in an easy-to-read booklet for your listening convenience.

The "Choozey Listener" will take the frustration and guesswork out of looking for your favorite music/radio station or playing the scanning game with your tuner and looking into stations you're not familiar with or don't want to listen to. Even when you leave a station's range, you could stay consistent with the format in the city you are traveling. You do not have to start all over again searching for something new to listen to with the "Choozey Listener," you will be able to tune in to the station of your choice at that very moment.

I would love to speak with you more about the "Choozey Listener." May I schedule an appointment for further discussion? I can be reached at the contact information above.

Thank you.

Sincerely,

Mack A. Parks, Jr.

I made contact with Hannah Ledford, the deputy commissioner over procurement and sales. I was amazed at how pleasant she was over the phone and her attention to detail as I explained what I had to offer. She sounded genuinely interested and told me to submit a procurement form along with my product and she would look at it. The word procurement threw me off. "What is that?" I asked. She explained to me what it was and I followed through.

After getting off the phone with her, I contacted my associates immediately and told them the good news. "We have got our foot in the door and they really like what they see," I said. What I really wanted to tell them was, "Hurry up! We got money to make!"

A few weeks had passed before my book cover was completed. It was nice. It had cars on the highway, billboards, exit ramps and trucks. Less than two weeks later, the book was complete. Each page was error free.

The radio stations were all lined up in their correct formats, no misspelled words and no offsets. It was perfect! What I had written freehand on notebook paper was professionally done. This is what I wanted. This was mine! I had finally put something together that people would want to buy! I did not know it would look like that. It was absolutely beautiful. I gave both of my associates a high five. They really came through.

When I took the cover and the prints to the local printer, they were impressed and excited for me. They even saw an opportunity for themselves if everything worked out right. I told them I just wanted 200 books printed to start with and if I get a large order, I'll be back for more. Well that sounded dandy and all, but that's not how printing works. They let me know up front that printers run on a certain count for a certain price. For instance, 200 books would cost the same as 500 books. The price doesn't get any lower just because you order less than the minimum. Hell, I wasn't ready for this because I didn't know 200 people. Whom was I going to sell 500 books to? I had no choice but to take it because I could not wait to show it off, and I was too tired to start all over searching for a better price.

"A person who won't read has no advantage over a person who can't read."

—Mark Twain

The Wake-Up Call

Three weeks passed before I would speak to Hannah Ledford again. I could not wait to see the look on her face when I walked into her office and showed her how professional my travel guide was. She would be so excited. I had a box of 200 travel guides that I wanted to sell that day! They were packed tight and neat. I held them as if they were custom ordered specifically for her office.

When I got to her office on Tuesday morning, the receptionist asked if I had an appointment. I said, "Yes," and she said, "Have a seat and I will let her know you're here." *I do not know why but every time I have an appointment with someone, I feel as though I am the only client scheduled for the day. I hate waiting!*

"Mr. Parks?"

"Yes."

"Ms. Hannah Ledford will see you now."

"Mack, come on in and have a seat. How you been doing?"

"Oh I've been doing great, Ms. Ledford. I must admit I'm a little excited about all the people who are going to be here for the games; the whole city is anxiously waiting."

"Yeah, you're right about that Mack. My office is in overdrive right about now. We are getting backed up because so many people are requesting information from our office."

"Let's see what you have, Mack. Oh, this is good."

(I am cheesing.)

GEORGIA

	ROCK	POP ROCK	URBAN R&B	JAZZ	TOP 40	OLDIES	COUNTRY	GOSPEL	RELIGIOUS	MEDIA	SPECIAL	PROGRAMS	SPANISH	EASY LISTENING
ALBANY														
(F.M.)														
WGPC 104.5	♦													
WJIZ 96.3			♦											
ATLANTA														
(F.M.)														
WKHX 90.7	♦													
WJCH 94.9	♦													
WZGC 92.9	♦													
WSB 98.5	♦									News				
WALL 93.3	♦									Sports				
WKLS 96.1		♦												
WRAS 88.5		♦												
WNNX 99.7		♦												
WAFJ 103.3			♦											
WEAS 104.7			♦											
WCLK 91.9			♦	♦		♦		♦						
WJZF 104.1				♦										
WRFG 92.1					♦									

-23-

"How many do you have?"

"I have a total of 500, but I brought 200 here today."

"Ok we can put 100 books in five different welcome centers for starters, and when they're all gone you can replenish them."

"That's great Ms. Ledford, thank you! I just charge $2 a book to help cover my expenses."

"Oh I'm sorry, Mack, but we don't buy the material that goes into the welcome centers. Publishers get permission from us to put their product into the welcome centers. You can put advertisements and sponsorships in the booklet to cover expenses."

Now I had a concerned look on my face before I asked her this next question. "Do you guys place the advertisements in the book?"

"No, you have to find the advertisers and the sponsors yourself. Just call around."

She said, "Just call around," as though I got the hook up. I did not know the first thing about advertisements or sponsorships. Who was going to sponsor me? I did not know anybody. Did my program look that good that it was just natural to think that I must have known about advertisers? Lady, are you kidding me? Wait a minute! Am I in over my head?

"Ok, Ms. Ledford, I can do that! So when I get the sponsors do I need to make another appointment with you, or do I take the books to the welcome centers myself?"

"No, Mr. Parks, all advertisements and sponsorships must be approved by us first. We have to make sure there is no alcohol, beer or cigarettes in the ads. Then we'll decide which welcome centers have the heaviest demand for radio stations."

"I understand, Ms. Ledford. That makes sense. Thank you for taking the time out to see me this morning." I extended my arm out to shake her hand and gently smiled and said, "I will get back to you within 30-45 days."

"Thank you for stopping by, Mr. Parks. Have a good day."

"You too!"

As I walked past the receptionist's desk with 200 books in my hands, I showed the look of confidence but felt the agony of defeat. *"What just happened in there?" "Did I blow it? Was I unprepared? What did I miss? I thought I had this locked up! Where do I go from here? What am I going to tell my associates — that I do not know what*

I am doing? I'll just be damned!"

No One Wants to Talk to an Amateur

Even though I felt defeated after I left Hannah Ledford's office, I still knew there was an opportunity out there, but it was hard for me to move on because I had put so much weight on myself to make the welcome centers a success. I tried contacting different ad agencies around town, but all of them told me they were booked with other clients. The Olympics were coming to town! The whole publishing industry is looking for sponsorship and advertising dollars. *How long would a catfish survive around sharks?* No one has ever heard of the "Choozey Listener" or Mack A. Parks Jr.!

Therefore, I thought to myself, I should focus my time and energy on Florida and make contact with AAA Motor Club. They are the most respected travel agency in the country. They always offer their customers discounts on certain products and give them benefits for being a valued member. It may be easier to do business in a less competitive environment.

I made contact with the marketing director at AAA. I cannot remember her name, but she was very open to my idea. In a very brief conversation, I introduced myself and told her what I had to offer and how it would benefit them and their customers and what I was looking for. I learned earlier from my previous conversations that if you do not have yourself together before you pick up that phone, your conversation is going to file 13 in a hurry *(the trash can!)*. No one wants to talk to an amateur.

She told me to send her a copy for review and she will get back with me within two weeks. Now here I was getting excited all over again just because someone offered to look at what I was proposing. I did not understand that this was only the process of building a relationship with a client. They deal with vendors all the time. Everyone thinks his or her product is what the market is looking for.

"Entrepreneurs are self made; you cannot coerce them into it."

—Mack A. Parks Jr.

I could not wait two weeks; I made contact with AAA after only one week. When I made contact with her office, she answered the phone and said, "How you doing, Mr. Parks?"

"I'm fine," I replied.

"I have your program here and I have a few questions for you. Radio stations change formats all the time, how will you be able to keep up with the changes?

"I am very aware of formats changing to meet the consumer demand, and that's why I developed a system so that I will be able to stay current with radio stations every six months," I said.

All I really said was that I am going to have to go back to the library and update every four months so that I will be ready for new material every six months. For the very first time I was questioned about whether I should have produced my book electronically or in print. If I had done this program on an electronic medium it would have been more expensive, but simpler to update.

"Ok, just to let you know we have a program where we test market new products from vendors before we put them before our customers. We want to make sure that it is something that piques their interest and has a demand. I am willing to put the "Choozey Listener" in our test market for 60 days to see where the potential lies. There are no guarantees that we will take this on; we're just giving this a shot at the market to see if it's a match for our customers."

"No problem! Thank you, thank you!"

"Ok, good luck, and we'll talk to you soon."

This is all I was looking for in the first place — an opportunity! She did not say one thing about advertising or sponsorship. It seems like I am always close to breaking wide open, but something always comes up at the last minute. Entrepreneurship is exciting, but it is not easy. I like the rush that I get and the possibilities if I hit. The thought of me riding around in a new convertible Bentley never escapes me. I will not let it! I want to be the first one in my entire family that has made the change from employee to entrepreneur. I want to be the first one to buy my parents a new home, car or RV, go on vacations without a six-month notice, pay cash for my niece's tuition, relieve the burdens and stress off my family so that they can enjoy the qualities of life. I want all the liberties and freedoms that corporate America does not offer.

"If your actions inspire others to dream more, learn more, do more and become more, you are a leader".

—John Quincy Adams

60 Percent of Something is Worth More Than 100 Percent of Nothing

Another opportunity is waiting for me around the corner. He is an attorney in Atlanta. A friend told him about my project, and he agreed to look at it. He had an office off Peachtree Street and seemed to be doing very well for himself. The truth is I really did not trust attorneys on the business side. To me attorneys only pacify you when they know they have an open and shut case and they are about to be paid. If they have to do any legwork, your fee just went up $300! I mean, come on!

I remember I paid $500 cash to an attorney to represent me on a suspended license case. This joker had me traveling all around town getting documents from the courthouse and bringing them back to him. As I was driving, I thought to myself, *"What the hell am I paying him for? I am the customer! Why am I burning all my fuel and spending all my time fetching what he needs?"*

I will not lie to you, I felt like a clown! I felt that the attorney should have done all the legwork. I was young and in trouble. In addition, when you have to go before a judge, you do not want any misunderstandings. I am not the incarcerated type! Do you understand me?

As I stepped into his office on the ninth floor, I received a warm welcome. When you are dealing with attorneys, they billed by the hour and small talk can be costly. I started the conversation with gratitude. "Thank you for seeing me on such short notice."

As I sat there and explained to him what I had to offer, he listened intently as to make sure I knew what I was talking about, which I liked that because I had his attention. When I was finished, he made me an offer.

He said, "I have a client that can use this magazine today. I can get you $60,000, but I get a 33 percent cut."

Here comes that attorney nightmare I had envisioned. I did not feel comfortable as we talked. My heart was not into what he was saying. I felt as though he was taking advantage of me, and I did not have a vote of confidence in his offer. I told him that I will get back in touch with him in the morning and we could draw up the paperwork. I never did call him back. He must have thought I was a real jackass. I went with my gut feeling. I really thought that 33 percent was excessive, and in the back of my mind, I was anticipating that the AAA experiment would come through, so I did not worry too much.

Six weeks had passed before I received a letter in the mail from AAA Motor Club. It read Dear, Mack Parks … I stopped reading. *You know those words of "thanks, but no thanks" that you get from a job interview. That is the feeling I had in my heart before I kept reading.* It said, "At this time, the 'Choozey Listener' is not a good fit for our customers from a marketing standpoint. We wish you the best of luck in your future endeavors. Sincerely, AAA Motor Club."

Damn! Here I go again.

Immediately I thought to call the attorney with the $60,000 offer. He did not respond back nor take my calls. Now I felt like a real jackass. It took me years to figure out the mess I had made. If you followed my story correctly, you may have pinpointed all of my errors. However, if you remember anything about this story, please remember this: 60 percent of something is worth more than 100 percent of nothing!

"The positive thinker sees the invisible, feels the intangible and achieves the impossible."

-Winston Churchill

The World Is Turning Green

One thing I have learned about products and the marketplace is that when it is your time to be in the right place at the right time, you had better be there! The market will not stand still. It waits for no one and it only has a spot for people who are ready.

I saw how satellite radio was making its way into the marketplace. I remember when satellite navigation systems were only installed in luxury vehicles; it was the hottest crave. People were not very familiar with satellite radio, but they knew it was coming and they knew it was expensive. The technology was there, the market was ready, and the people took out their wallets. Today we have satellite DJs and news anchors with $500 million contracts. Who would have thought that Rush Limbaugh, Howard Stern, Sean Hannity, CNN, Fox News, ESPN, The Weather Channel, Wall Street Report, etc., would create an entire new market of listeners?

When I look back at the "Choozey Listener," I wish I had done some things differently. Clearly, my judgments were based upon emotion and not sound business decisions. I am not alone when I talk about this. I have heard other entrepreneurs speak about the same thing. However, I do not want the next entrepreneur to experience the agony of defeat. You will experience some learning curves because that is just a part of entrepreneurship. However, I do not want you to lose thousands of dollars just because you have a bad feeling.

The corrections that I learned from my previous experience were placed on the business side of this book. I found out the truth of where I went wrong. It is not over! God is not done with me yet. I simply call this a lesson learned. I have to keep moving!

Remember when I told you that I have 18 years of experience in the transportation industry? Well those years were not in vain, my friend. I saw an opportunity that no one else was paying attention to; I stared at it for over eight months because I just knew someone had already moved on it. However, when I went and inquired on the subject, there was no answer!

"Do you provide any service to your clients that rent P.O. Boxes?"

"Huh?" They did not even understand what I was asking.

"No sir, we just have the customer fill out a P.O. Box registration, and they rent the box for six or 12 months at a time." This cannot be true, can it?

You mean to tell me that you let a paying customer walk around aimlessly for six months to a year without ever contacting him or keeping in touch. Nowadays if you have a paying customer, you want to keep them happy. It is cheaper to keep a customer than it is to find a new one. Here I go again! I found something that no one else was looking at. One thing that I have noticed about myself is that I do not think small. I think big! Nevertheless, I break it down to small pieces so I can see it and understand it better. People tell me all the time that I do not understand the impact that I will have on people's lives because of what I am proposing. Nevertheless, I do not concentrate on the scope of the project. I just see an opportunity and try to capitalize on it. Can you imagine having 1,000 customers and only corresponding with them once every six months? Doesn't that sound insane? I would be afraid that someone else might offer them something different. This is where the excitement begins when you start thinking of ways to bring new products and services to the market. That is what entrepreneurship is! I absolutely love this!

The transportation industry is a trillion dollar industry. *$1 trillion*! Do you know how much 1 percent of $1 trillion is? Do you know how much 1 percent of $1 billion is? OMG! I am getting nervous! Why can't they see what I see? Are they looking too hard? Are they taking their customers for granted? Are they not paying attention? Are they too busy buying one another out? Do they not see the digital landscape? What is it? Am I lucky?

I see people wasting time and money because they are not being served properly. I see people wasting time and money on doing things they do not want to do. Customers are looking for ways to use their time more wisely. I see customers frustrated by making unnecessary trips to handle their business or being under-served. I see people on cell phones all day. I see how unlimited texting has become the norm. For some folks, time has become more valuable than money. Wait a minute! I believe that I can solve the million-dollar question: How much will people *pay* to resolve their frustrations and regain their quality of life? Let's face it: time is a precious commodity. Once it is gone, that is it! It will never come back. *Wow*! I see a service that I could fulfill! I see how technology can influence people's lives. I see people using their time more wisely and using resources more efficiently. Wait a minute! OMG! I see a green economy headed my way.

Below is a letter that I wrote to the U.S. Postmaster General about my business venture:

Mr. Jack E. Potter

Postmaster General & CEO of USPS

United States Government

475 L'Enfant Plaza S.W.

Washington, D.C. 20260

My name is Mack A. Parks Jr., CEO of Instant Notification Systems Inc. in Atlanta, Ga. I am an entrepreneur and a veteran and thus, very concerned about my country and the current economy. Most pointedly, I have specific concerns about the well-being of the United States Postal Service (USPS). I was urged to contact you directly in response to a CNN report that requested entrepreneurs to share any new ideas and/or cutting-edge technology to assist the USPS in achieving a more substantial market share over its competitors. I welcome the opportunity to provide external services to the USPS that will include eliminating USPS expense issues and substantially increase its profit margins.

We have developed a technology product and service that I believe would be a quantifiable asset to the USPS. It is called E-POMS (Electronic Post Office Messaging Service). I have introduced my product and service to the larger community by conducting several targeted surveys. My results indicate that customers are willing to pay for E-POMS and verify that they need this service to be more productive and efficient. Furthermore, I have conducted research using a base number of 200 post offices and substantiated a potential of over $3 million in new revenue that will not include an increase of stamp costs.

Ever since 2001, the number of USPS career employees has decreased by 20 percent. This year alone, 40,000 positions have been reduced. It is my understanding that several USPS offices are under review for consolidation. We firmly believe that E-POMS have the potential to reduce or, in some cases, eliminate consolidation of the USPS retail offices. The growth plan for the USPS states that the USPS desires to achieve revenue growth in 2016, 2019, and 2024 and beyond. We believe E-POMS can help you achieve this!

The status quo simply will not do! With over 36,000 retail locations and over 75 billion deliveries (nearly half the world's mail), we understand that the USPS must have the ability to leverage logistics, distribution and retail networks in order to create new revenue for the 21st century. Long-term success requires fundamental legislative change. In the short-term, we believe E-POMS can help significantly.

In the words of USPS spokesperson Judy de Torok, "Our goal is to have U.S. mail remain relevant to the American public.... For us the challenge is, how do we continue to reach customers in the electronic world?"

Mr. Potter, I believe the USPS has a grand opportunity. Collaborating with E-POMS and utilizing innovative technology to improve upon the current service with little effort can provide a win-win for everyone involved — especially the USPS customers.

I look forward to hearing from you and would certainly welcome an opportunity to meet with you in person to discuss E-POMS and its capability in further detail. Please feel free to contact me directly at 404.XXX-XXX (cell) or at

mparks@my-epoms.com

Thank You.

Mack A. Parks Jr.

DAVID SCOTT
13TH DISTRICT, GEORGIA

WWW.HOUSE.GOV/DAVIDSCOTT

DAVID.SCOTT@MAIL.HOUSE.GOV

COMMITTEE ON
AGRICULTURE

COMMITTEE ON
FINANCIAL SERVICES

COMMITTEE ON
FOREIGN AFFAIRS

Congress of the United States
House of Representatives
Washington, DC 20515–1013

July 12, 2010

Mr. Mack Arthur Parks, Jr.
4031 Heritage Crossing Point Southwest
Hiram, Georgia 30141

Dear Mack:

I received an update from the United States Postal Service that your paperwork has been received and being reviewed.

Your Constituent Services Representative, Sheila Davis is monitoring the progress of your case.

I will let you know as soon as I receive any information from the agency.

Thank you for the opportunity to serve you.

Sincerely,

David Scott
Member of Congress

DS: sd

WASHINGTON OFFICE
225 Cannon House Office Building
Washington, DC 20515-1013
Phone: (202) 225-2939
Fax: (202) 225-4628

JONESBORO OFFICE
173 North Main Street
Jonesboro, GA 30236
Phone: (770) 210-5073
Fax: (770) 210-5673

SMYRNA OFFICE
888 Concord Road, Ste. 100
Smyrna, GA 30080
Phone: (770) 432-5405
Fax: (770) 432-5813

UNITED STATES
POSTAL SERVICE

The Honorable David Scott
Member of Congress
Attention: Sheila Davis
173 North Main Street
Jonesboro, GA 30236-3567

Dear Congressman Scott:

This is in response to your inquiry on behalf of Mack A. Parks, Jr. It is my pleasure to be of assistance.

We appreciate your interest in assisting Mr. Parks and for the opportunity to address his concerns. It is my understanding that Mr. Parks has developed a new technological product and service entitled Electronic Post Office Notification (e-PON) and wants to share his proposal with the Postal Service.

The Postal Service always welcomes the opportunity to explore new ideas and is continually searching for ways to improve our operations. Therefore, we have created the **Unsolicited Proposal Program** to give companies and entrepreneurs the option of sharing their best ideas. Mr. Parks may obtain information by accessing our web site at www.usps.com and select the link to **About USPS & News** (located in upper right corner). He will then scroll down and select **Doing Business with Us**. From this page, Mr. Parks will select **Suppliers**. After which, he will scroll down again and select **Unsolicited Proposal Program**. This page will advise Mr. Parks to see Publication 131 for complete information about the program.

Please be assured that Mr. Parks' idea involving e-PON will receive careful consideration and we appreciate him taking the time to contact us.

If I may be of further assistance in other postal matters, please do not hesitate to contact my office.

Sincerely,

Kate F. Wiley
District Manager
Atlanta District

Vision

When I began my journey into prosperity, one of the first doors I had to break through is called "NOISIV." I have never seen this sign before so I did not quite understand the language. It sounded Swedish, but I was not sure so I had to make some adjustments.

Let me ask you a question: On your way to work, have you ever gotten into your car on a chilly morning, started the engine, buckled your seat belt, put the car in reverse and then realized that the back windshield was frosted? Didn't that irk you? Then you had to get out of the car, scrape off the ice and defrost the windshield, correct? After that, you were well on your way to where you were going. Well it is the same thing in business.

You already know in your mind where you want to go, but sometimes you cannot see how to get there. You have to make some adjustments. First, you need a business plan. This is very essential. It is the same thing as having a map for when you go on vacation. I do realize that maps already have the roads paved out for you, and all you have to do is follow the route you want to take. This is where I help you design your map, the business plan. During this process, I will show you examples of my business plan so that you will have a personal feeling of what is being discussed. This is not hard. Follow me. Beginning right now, I want you to start thinking about the vision you have for your company. You have to set your mind up right and start thinking like an entrepreneur and leave the employee mindset at the job. The journey into prosperity is not as simple as you might have imagined. You are going to have to get yourself prepared and move some things out of the way. You will not waltz your way through this process because you are going to have to *"do the things that other people won't do, so you can have the things that other people won't have."* After I understood the inner message that was going on inside my head, I went back to the door of prosperity, turned the sign around and it read, *"Vision."* Then I paused and asked myself, "What do I see?"

Before we go any further, I want you to be mentally prepared to put *all* your cards on the table. We are going to empty our minds of *everything that* we think we know about business. I want to know what has been holding you back: procrastination, fear of success, waiting for your retirement or perhaps a good, swift kick in the butt? I say that jokingly because there are so many people who think like you and do not understand that the marketplace is full of successful people who are making money with less intelligence than YOU have. Our business plan is going to start with several topics that will explain what we are doing and why. We will identify your *vision, mission, target market, strategy, marketing objectives* and *cost*. First, we are going to understand what vision means to you! To do this, we are going to do a little exercise. The results are uniquely yours. No one else can visualize what you see in the picture. What other people see may not resonate with you. This is your personal connection to your customers. You are your own boss here. Whatever your answers are, this is who you are. There are no *wrong* answers.

So let us begin. For each photo on the following pages, write whatever comes to your mind when you look at the picture:

The answers that you wrote are what your customers, suppliers, partners and bankers are going to see. This is who you are. You will represent your product or service from day one.

Our first step in this process is to write *your* vision on paper for the product or service that you will offer. This is a very important part of your program. Remember to put *all* your cards on the table. Do not worry if it sounds silly or not. The more we get out of you in the beginning, the more options we will have to work with at the end. We will find out very shortly if your business will make money. If it does not, we will go with that other project that is floating around in your head.

Please understand that customers are waiting on *you*! They cannot wait to buy your new product or service. They have been looking for it but cannot find it because it is stuck in your head. Isn't this a great position to be in?

Sometimes we have to see things before they appear. I call this faith. Have you ever had the experience of saying what you want aloud and six months to a year later, you had it? That is because you put it out there in the universe to find you. Speak loud and often of what you expect. Success is not quiet. Whatever you are looking for, it is looking for you!

Now visualize what your business looks like. Get a mental picture and write down everything about your company that we are about to build. Is it a two-story building or 40-story building? How many floors will it have? Where will it be located? What is the name of your company? How many employees will you have? What is motivating you to start a business? Which bank will you build a relationship with and why? What does your business offer? How do your customers benefit from your product or service? Describe your customers. Do they walk, catch the bus, drive a car or catch a plane? Are they blue collar or white collar? All of the information that is in your head has value. Please understand that you have to see it in your mind before you invest your time in it.

"If you have to persuade a person to become an entrepreneur, then he or she is not an entrepreneur."

—Mack A. Parks Jr.

Below is my vision that I will use to help grow my business:

(Example) Instant Notification's Vision Statement:

To transcend the global mail service into an electronic medium that uses E-POMS (Electronic Post Office Messaging Service) as a primary source for determining mail pickup. E-POMS is partly purposed on a green initiative to reduce carbon buildup in our communities. Similar purposes in our communities are served by car-pooling programs and best practices. E-POMS serve to eliminate wasteful carbon toxic exposure and fuel expenditures caused by making unnecessary visits to post office boxes. To reduce carbon footprint one-step at a time. By doing so, we want to be partly built on a green platform that allows us to use renewable energies in our systems and infrastructures. We want to be centrally located in downtown Atlanta near the Georgia Tech campuses so that we are able to stay current with renewable technologies and recruit the top talents in the field, much like how Apple does with Stanford University. This will give us the ability to transcend the global mail service.

"A delayed success is better than an on time failure."

—Ted Turner

Mission

A mission statement is a fundamental goal that will set the tone for the quality of your business; where a set of principles that you practice to attract and retain customers. It is an important part for your business because it shows that you are in deep thought of how you want to nurture and grow your business. It should be defined by the perception that you created.

Al Davis, former owner of the Oakland Raiders NFL team had a very short mission statement for his ball club: "Just Win, Baby." That is all he paid attention to, winning! Facebook is up and running 24/7 and 365 days a year. What do you think Facebook CEO Mark Zuckerberg's mission statement would be? I believe it's "We will not fail our customers" and the weight of this company is being held together by a mission statement that he believes in and implement throughout his company.

What do you think Google's mission statement would be? They have a customer base across the globe as well. When the founders of the company put their plan together, what were they thinking? What did they set out to do? You must ask these questions yourself. Whatever passions you put out on the market is what customers are going to believe in. What about Apple Inc? What did Steve Jobs envision before the world could see what was coming? His passion to bring new products to the market with no flaws has earned my trust. I buy Apple because I never have any flaws with their products and I never worry about viruses. Was this a mission statement that Apple set out to accomplish? Maybe.

After reviewing the mission statements from the companies that I just mentioned, my mission statement for this book became clearer.

1. Lay out six easy steps to prepare your business for the marketplace.

2. Raise your confidence and empower your mindset.

3. Add fuel to your fire so that you will succeed.

What is your mission statement? What is that one thing that you will deliver that would make your customers keep coming back? I have to be honest with you, when I first started laying my foundation down for my business, I did not know what a mission statement was either. I did not even know why it was necessary to put on paper. My mission was clear in my head! *"Quit my job, open a business and make a lot of money!"* That is all I could come up with; I was going to fumble my way into prosperity. That was my pathway to success. I did not understand the basic steps to prosperity. I did not know it was this simple. I was operating on pure adrenalin. I knew I had something within me to prosper, but I did not know what business I wanted to get into or why I wanted to get into it. Real estate sounded good. You could make a lot of money in it. However, the thought of me driving around looking at beautiful homes is relaxing to me. It inspires me. I did not want to turn my dreams into a job. Consulting work sounds like a lucrative business. My friends in California are making a comfortable living at it. Whom would I consult? My background does not have a need for consulting. My background deals with applications and interviews.

Opening a sports bar sounds great! I love eating out with family and friends and having a good time. I had to ask myself, am I the type of person that likes to cook all day and clean up at night seven days a week? Not! I have to be honest with myself. I do not want another job or a business that acts like a job. I want a business that makes money whether I am in the office or not. Following in someone else's footsteps may not be profitable for me. The only thing that I could put my time, money and energy into is a service or product that I created myself. (See Instant Notification's mission statement below.)

(Example) Instant Notification's Mission Statement:

The mission of Instant Notification (IN) is to bridge the gap of dissatisfaction between our clients and their customers by providing them with powerful software tools that save them time and money. E-POMS is our first product, and it aligns with our mission statement. Time is something no one can ever recoup. It is valuable to a customer, company or individual. Money is a precious resource that no one can afford to waste. Communication is the key that opens new markets. IN wants to be a part of that. Our integrity is built into this belief. We will build value by gaining our customers' trust. Information is the currency of tomorrow. We understand what it takes to build relationships and secure a customer trust. E-POMS will be recognized as a sophisticated work of efficiency. Customers and consumers will recognize our service as an organizational tool that they will use every day. We bring value to our clients by bringing people closer together, and bringing people closer together makes for a healthier economy.

Target Market

What is a target market, and what does it have to do with what I am doing? This is a subject that many entrepreneurs are familiar with but do not understand how it applies to their business. Target marketing is identifying the right customers for your business. I remember when I first started out in business; my consultant asked me, "Who is your target audience?" I said, "Everybody!" All I had on my mind was making money and selling to whoever buys. This is not how it works.

We see target marketing every day in our lives. It is in the neighborhood you live in, your place of work, the restaurants you frequent, and your favorite entertainment complex. For every establishment that you like to go to frequently, you are considered a part of that particular target market. Before that establishment opened, they knew your age, sex and income. This information gives them insight of who their customers will be.

This is important because it keeps you from wasting a lot of time and money. Trying to attract *everybody* is not a good idea. Let me tell you why. First, let me ask you some questions: Would it make sense to you to market beef products to a vegetarian? Wouldn't you say that is a waste of your time and theirs? Would Mercedes Benz put a dealership around $50,000 homes? Of course not! That is because that neighborhood does not fit the profile of such a luxury car buyer. Why waste your time spending money on a customer that cannot afford your product? Does this make sense to you?

You want your customers tailor-made to fit your business. Think about the restaurants that you go to frequently. Now think about the one you go to every now and then. The restaurant that you go to frequently is within your target market range (budget), say, $18-$32 for a meal. That particular business has just what your wallet is looking for. Now the upscale restaurant that is located outside your proximity may have a menu that starts out at $55 a meal. You go every now and then to this one. That is fine. They appreciate your business, but they are not targeting you because you do not fit the profile or income level that they are seeking.

Businesses survive because they have customers who frequent them regularly. That is how they stay afloat. Customers that come by every now and then or on special occasions are not what they are putting all of their marketing and advertising dollars towards.

Shopping malls do the same thing, too. I often hear people say, "Why don't they put a shopping mall like this on our side of town? I'm tired of driving way over here to get a nice dress." Well, that shopping mall near you is the one that caters to your budget. Your dollars help sustain that community and the business owners. That dress that you like to buy every now and then will not sustain a business or a community. Your spending habit is too slow. Businesses locate market and advertise to their customer base. These customers can afford the product or service on a daily basis. This is what we must do as well. We must divulge all of our time and energy to focus on finding the right customers that will sustain our business. Like many entrepreneurs, I did not understand the mechanics of finding the right customer. I am the one who was trying to sell beef to a vegetarian. Wasting my time and theirs trying to convince them that it will not disturb their diet. This is why I believe Facebook may become the world's most powerful tool because it has specific data that businesses would use to identify their customers.

Below, write a paragraph about your target market. Explain in detail who they are and what they do, such as education level, gender, age, income level, marital status, children, etc. Get as much information about your customers as you can. This will help you launch your business quicker and easier.

_____

_____

_____

_____

_____

_____

_____

_____

_____

_____

_____

(Example) Instant Notification's Target Market:

The companies below are the original customers that we feel are best suited to fit our business model that we are trying to create. We feel that in going after these potential customers, we will fulfill our niche in the marketplace. The Postal Industry is a $1 trillion industry. The USPS is the main core of this market. This industry has many moving parts, but we are focusing on the P.O. Box customers. We are focusing on public and private sectors of this market.

This market has been under-served for decades. Saving time, energy and money are the ultimate reasons why this opportunity exists. Creating customer satisfaction through a *green consumer initiative* will create sustainable profits with astute stewardship.

A. United States Post Office, 38 Million in the United States
B. Pak Mail Corporation, 500 U.S. locations
C. Post Net Corporation, 445 U.S. locations
D. Mail It Corporation, 100 U.S. Locations
E. Mail Boxes Etc., 4,300 U.S. locations, owned and operated by United Parcel Service (UPS)
F. Going Postal

Research

I would like to bring something to your attention in the name of research. Whatever product or service you intend to offer your customers, it is attached to an industry. There is nothing new under the sun. It does not matter if you are baking cupcakes or changing motor oil, it is part of an industry. I have noticed many first time entrepreneurs who have spent countless resources and energy on their product only to find out that someone else is doing the same thing. However, that is Ok; competition is great! It actually helps the economy grow. However, if it is your first time venturing out into the marketplace, this could be a blow to your mindset. Don't fret. This is a common mistake with most entrepreneurs. There still may be an opportunity that you can capitalize on. It is extremely important to do some careful research before you extend yourself and waste valuable resources. By researching your industry, you can find out much more than what you are looking for. You will find things like demographics, wholesale costs, latest trends, customers' buying habits, delivery systems, suggested retail pricing, future business models and so much more. By conducting thorough research, you gain a competitive edge because you can see which way the market is going. Once you gain knowledge of your industry then you can start to adjust your business plans accordingly. The slightest detail could be the difference between success and failure.

Keeping an eye on your competitor and your cost could lead you to stable profitability. Case in point, there were two restaurants that were within three blocks of one another that were soliciting the same customers. One was a seafood restaurant and the other was a steak and seafood restaurant. They both operated seven days a week. Their menus were slightly different, but their prices were very competitive. There was not much room for profit on both sides. Therefore, the seafood owner did a little bit of research within his business and found out that his busiest days were Wednesday through Saturday. Therefore, he focused on the days where he made the most money and realigned his staff and business model. His new business model was "Open Wednesday – Thursday, 5 p.m. – 11 p.m., and Friday – Saturday, 5 p.m. – 2 a.m. This realignment proved to be extremely successful! Three things happened right away. 1) Overhead costs went down 30 percent. Utilities were not in use three days out of the week. That is 12 days a month, which really adds up over a period of time. 2) Standing room only! By opening up at 5 p.m. during the weekday, people started lining up outside the door around 4:15 – 4:30 to get a good seat. To passers-by it gave the illusion that something special was going on inside. It created a buzz around the community and piqued people's interest. 3) Sales went up 21 percent. That is because whenever people are happy and having a good time, *they spend money*!

One of the most powerful tools to use for research is the Internet. Instantaneously you can find almost anything at your fingertips. Google, Bing and Yahoo are your biggest providers on the Internet to find information on subjects that pique your interest. However, if you are not having success on the Internet, your local library has everything you need. A very powerful and useful tool is free to the public. There you will find tons of information that is centered around your industry. Reference books, study guides, industry news, trade magazines and yearly data.

COMPETITION

You may not think so but competition is good for the marketplace. It drives innovation that inspires motivation. It puts people to work and develops organizations. Do not think that you are the only one with a good idea. Someone else is thinking about it too! In business, you are going to have competitors and/or copycats. In fact, the shear presence of competition raises the bar just a little higher. We are competitive by nature. It lives within us. Do you remember when you were a kid and you came to school wearing a fresh pair of All-Stars? Then the next day someone else came in with a fresh pair, but in a different color. It is the same thing in business. No one wants to be outdone. You have to live on a competitive edge.

Nevertheless, not all businesses are your competitors. If you own a dry cleaner for instance, you do not have to worry about the coffee shop next door siphoning off your sales. Are you with me? Many businesses will be irrelevant to your business. If you owned a motorcycle dealership and it sits across the street from a day care center, you have little worry about the parents becoming bike riders. However, if you are planning to open a donut shop, please do not put it next door to the coffee shop. No one will make money! You are moving directly next to a competitor. Does this make sense?

Have you ever seen three barbershops operating on the same block? What in the world are they thinking? Who is making money? I mean, you have three barbers fighting for the same head. What is going to happen next? One of the barbers is going to lower the price. Well guess what, the next barber is going to follow suit and then everybody is going to have to lower his or her price. This is not good business. You might as well go get a job. Every time I see this, I ask myself, *"Who's going to fold first?"* If you are in the presence of this situation, get them a copy of this book.

Determining your competition is a very simple task. Companies that offer the same type of product that you offer are considered competitors. If their real estate is overlapping yours with the same price points, they are a competitor.

I have mainly focused on physical competition, brick and mortar. We must be on the lookout for cyber competition as well. Research is a must in every business, whether it is online or a physical locality. I disregarded researching my industry and it cost me. I only concentrated my efforts on what I could see locally; I was not thorough enough on the Internet. I thought that since I could not see it on the streets, it did not exist on the Internet. I was wrong! This goes back to one of my personal proverbs: Just because you do not believe it, does not mean it is not happening.

One of the biggest mistakes I made was diving right in without looking at the landscape that I was approaching. I knew the company that I was putting together had an 80 percent chance for success in the marketplace. I even gave it a name. I got a logo and business cards for the company and my staff. I was thrilled with the new design and the way the name sounded when I told people. When I sat and talked with my mentor about my new name and logo, she asked me was my name and logo trademarked or copyrighted? I said, "Not yet!" She then said, "Let's do some research to see if anyone else has this name." *Bam*! There it was. A company from Ohio had a trademark on the name that I wanted to put on my product. I was devastated. My thrill was diminished because I felt I had the perfect name for the perfect product. However, I was even more upset when I realized that my investment had been wasted. I thought about the $600 that I spent for the design and business cards for my staff. I felt foolish. When I add it all up, I call it a lesson learned.

Whatever business you desire to get into, do thorough research on that industry so that you do not waste dollars, time or energy reinventing the wheel. After all, you want to make a name for yourself that you will not have to share with anyone else.

OBJECTIVES

Objectives are very specific tasks to complete your goal. Remember when you were a kid and your mom said, "You can't go outside and play until the house is clean." You instantly knew what she wanted accomplish. That meant you had to sweep and mop the kitchen floor, wash the dishes, take out the garbage, vacuum the living room, clean the bathroom, clean out your closet, make up your bed and dust the furniture. These are all objectives. They are tasks that when completed will accomplish the goal. This is what it took to clean the house. A lot of our business knowledge has already been taught to us. We just do not recall it. After you have completed all of the objectives, you were able to go outside and play. In business, your plan objectives should be specific goals that can be measured. I want to pause right here because I can hear my mom's voice in the back of my mind telling me, "*It shouldn't take you all day to clean up your room.*" Was this a *specific* task that could be measured? Was mom a proprietor of the home? Did she understand the time frame for each chore to be completed? Keep your list to three or four tasks because a long list makes it harder to keep your focus. The difference from what mom taught us and how the business world operates is that she did not say clean the house by 12:30 or by the end of the month. She said before you go outside to play. Nevertheless, if you did not care about going outside, you cleaned the house at your leisure. This attitude is a recipe for disaster in the business community.

When I read the definition of objectives in the business arena, it became clear to me what I was missing when I was putting together the "Choozey Listener Radio Travel Guide."

If I had specific goals in mind *before* I started running all over the place, I would have had a better chance for success. As the saying goes, "When you know better, you will do better!"

Some of you may have gotten lost as I did when I first read the words *objectives* in a business sentence. I asked my mentor, "What do you mean? *Specific goals that can be measured? Huh?"* It took me awhile to put it together because I had to see it as it applied to what I was doing.

One of the best scenarios for me to describe is the conversation I had with a friend who wanted to throw herself a 40th birthday party. Let's say that in January, Bianca decided she wanted to throw herself a red carpet 40th birthday party in June. It would be a sit-down dinner by invitation only. She wanted to have all her friends, family and former elementary school teachers present. She also wanted to have it at an exclusive location, like a country club. She envisioned everyone dressed in formal attire, sequined dresses and tuxedos or suits, like at the Oscar Awards! The invitations would resemble those of a royal wedding — purple, white and gold. Guests would pull up to the front door for valet parking and walk into the venue under a white canopy with red carpet. Appetizers and socializing would be in one room and a sit-down dinner would be in another. There would be chandeliers hanging from the ceiling, servers dressed in black and white, walking around serving cocktails and hors d'oeuvres, soft music playing in the background and a gorgeous view overlooking the city. Of course, white linen sheets would drape the dinner tables, and candles would accent the atmosphere while guests relaxed at an open bar, enjoying appetizers offered on sterling silver platters. Delicacies would lie on tables decorated with custom-cut ice sculptures, a Miss America crown on one-table and stiletto shoes on another. Classy champagne glasses and jasmine-scented flowers would decorate the tables with a professional photographer capturing the moment. This would be the party of the year!

When she finished talking to me about this party, she did not realize that she had parts of a business plan. She had vision, mission, target market, and *objectives* that were *measurable*.

Her *vision* was the description of what you just read. Her *mission* was to make this the party of the year. Her *target market* was her friends and family.

Her *objectives* were:

1. Give a time frame to complete the mission (six months, January – June). This is the part that is measurable because she is giving herself a time frame to be completed. She should have something completed out of her vision every month. Measurables give you deadlines and the opportunity to track your progress. If she did not make her objectives measurable, and then she would just daydream and lollygag all the way up until May, then try to make all pieces of her puzzle fit together in 30 days. Her mission would have little chance of success.

2. Find a location. Where could she find an exclusive venue that overlooks the city and offers all the amenities and accommodations she desired?

3. Decide which friends and relatives will be invited to the party.

4. Decide on a budget.

That is it! Her conversation was long but her objectives were short. Remember: you want to keep it short so that you will not lose focus on what you are doing.

Likewise, the objectives for my business were also concise:

1. Develop a wireless technology model for E-POMS by Jan. 5.

2. Protect our technology in the marketplace.

3. Introduce my company to potential clients.

4. Brand us as the No. 1 leader in electronic mail delivery.

"Never let your minimums become your maximum."

—Robert Dean Jr.

STRATEGY

In my point of view, the difference between winning and losing is *strategy* — how you approach the situation. You strategize to accomplish the overall goal. Whether it is a good or a bad one, you *must* have one. I do not think there is a bad strategy for any entrepreneur because entrepreneurship is uncharted territory. You just have to really think about the best way for you to succeed at what you are doing. If you knew where all the pitfalls were, success would be much easier. However, this is not the case. First, you must think about the landscape that you are venturing into such as what obstacles in your way are preventing you from winning.

I love to use sports and politics as an analogy to express my point of view. It is one of the best scenarios known to man. In the world of sports, strategy is the ultimate recipe for success. In the game of football, it consists of height, weight, size and strength. If you are a coach on the opposing team, you are looking at ways to dominate the opponent. For instance, if your players outweigh the other team, your strategy may be to run the ball the majority of the game because the opposing team does not have enough weight to stop you. Can you imagine 6'5", 350-pound linemen lined up against 6'2", 200-pound linemen?

Another example would be in the world of politics. One of the best strategies in the history of politics was unveiled in the 2012 U.S. Presidential campaign. The sitting president was up against a $400 million war chest. His Republican opponent was well funded and well rehearsed. The President's strategy to regain the White House was to: 1) Concentrate on eight states that had the most electoral votes in the union. 2) Introduced his opponent in a negative light *before* he introduced himself. 3) Establish 150 field offices in each state, and 4) then fly back and forth between cities delivering a message that says, "Republicans are against the working middle class." These strategies worked perfectly. The President was elected to a second term by a large margin. It even gained his campaign strategist a nod for the political Hall of Fame. Strategy is all about using the best methods to get your product to the end user. (*Your customers*)

MARKETING

Why is marketing so important? "Can't I just run an ad on cable television?" I get asked this question from time to time. The answer is "yes." If you are selling Pee-Wee Herman Pet Blankets for $19.99, buy one get one free! Cable television is not the answer for everything. I see toy products for children between the ages of 6 and 11 years old being advertised at 11 p.m. Is this the best way to reach that audience? Cable television is only one strategy mechanism to reach your audience. Marketing is important!

Marketing is all about putting your product or service in the hands of potential customers. That is it! After we identify and pinpoint our potential customers (target market), how will we reach them? Where will they be? How will they get your product?

You have to develop a strategy to maximize your time and money in order to achieve your objective, which is making money! This will be a constant review of your customers' likes, dislikes and habits.

Wherever your customers are, your business should be right in front of them. If they are going to the moon, then your sign should be on the space shuttle! Do you understand me? You must constantly remind them what a great product you have. Even as I am writing this book, I am constantly reminding myself of who my customers are, where they are and how I will reach them.

My customers can be effectively marketed via the Internet, networking events, the Chamber of Commerce, self-development seminars or Small Business Administration orientations.

Social media marketing is very effective. Thousands of entrepreneurs are using Twitter and Facebook to grow their businesses. Learn to use them to your advantage. Both have a demographic profile of over 500 million people and businesses. These are customers that you are trying to reach.

How you market is what contributes to the bottom line. Marketing affects sales, public relations, packaging and distribution. Did you know that Virginia Slim Gold cigarettes have the same tobacco as Virginia Slim Light? In addition, the Virginia Slim Ultra is the same cigarette as the Virginia Slim Silver. They are selling the same tobacco to different customers because of how they market it to them. Let me ask you a question. Do you notice that a 22 oz. T-Bone only cost you $25 when you go out to the local steakhouse, but when you go to the Japanese steakhouse, that same meat cost you $49. Why is that? It is not necessarily bigger or better; it is how they marketed it to you. The $25 steak says, "Come hungry and stay late, we're just around the corner." The $49 steak says, "Come dine with us and unwind with that special someone in your life." Neither one of these ads said anything about the steak, but it affects the bottom line of your business.

Let me ask you some more questions: Do you ever notice the packaging on cereal boxes? Do you see how the national brand is always out front with vibrant colors, and the store brand is always in the back on the bottom? However, did you notice that the ingredients of the contents are the same? The same product that is packaged differently gets a better price.

One of the most important things that every entrepreneur should keep their focus on is *their* customer base, not everybody. Not everybody wants what you have, nor do they need what you have.

However, the customer that you do attract, they want everything you have.

Have you ever noticed the guy jogging around the park with the Nike warm-up suit? Did you notice that he also had on Nike sneakers, Nike socks, Nike shirt and a Nike hat? He wants everything that Nike has! These are the type of customers you want for your business. We retain these customers through rewards programs, special offers, one-day sales and discounts. While you are showing them your appreciation, they will be coming back to buy out the store.

Put your marketing dollars where they belong. This piece of the puzzle will save you money, while making you money.

"Happiness lies not in the mere possession of money; it lies in the joy of achievement, in the thrill of creative effort."

— Franklin D. Roosevelt

COST

What is your cost? I saved the very best for last. Cost is a subject that infuriates entrepreneurs and discourages them because they think that what they are embarking on is something that is unattainable — that is simply not true. This is the point where they quit before they get started. We tend to think that everything is all about cost. Nevertheless, if you do not know what you are doing or where you are going from a business standpoint, what difference does it make how much it costs. No one is going to give you a loan or invest in your company if you do not have a clue what you are doing. You have to make your business plan definitive and attractive, not with cute designs or flashy projection slides, but by using real-time data and numbers.

I want to tell you a personal story. When I was creating my business plan for my company, I was using artificial numbers to support my vision because I did not want to stand out too far from my peers who were taking the same class that I was. The funding for their business plans called for $23,000 to $75,000. I wanted to stay in line with them because I thought they would frown at me if I said what I really needed. So I stated that I needed $95,000 to support my business plan, but when I punched $95,000 into my calculations, it spit out negative results. I was in the red before I got started. My business plan could not work on a $95,000 investment. The numbers just did not add up. I knew what the problem was though. I did not use *real-time* data. I learned by experience that you could not guess what your cost will be. I stated earlier in my start-up cost analysis that my equipment and supplies were around $200, 000, not including salary and rent. My actual business plan called for $2 million. Where am I going to get this type of money? I felt somewhat standoffish because my project demanded so much more than my peers did. In actuality, they were happy for me. They knew that I was embarking on something that had never been done. I was holding myself back. Still I had to find courage to ask an investor to invest $2 million in me when I never made $100,000 in my life! When the time came to make my pitch, I was trying to use big words, metaphors, pie charts and shined shoes to make me look and sound good. What I found out was that it was not necessary because my numbers supported the business plan. I was relieved and thankful because one of the investors said, "$2 million sounds about right! I can't wait to see it." She said this with confidence because she saw what I had in my *vision;* she understood my *mission*; she liked my *target market;* and she loved my *strategy.* *Cost* became a nonissue because the presentation was well thought out, presented clearly, the data was accurate and the numbers supported it. As a result, I have some exciting news to share with you: During the time this book was printed, my legal team has notified me that the first round of funding has been approved.

At this point I want you to get a pen and paper and write down *all* of your estimated expenses for 30 days (1month), including toilet paper. Remember at the beginning of the book that I said you are going to find out whether your business is viable or not? In addition, if not, you will go with that other idea you have floating around in your head. Well this is that time.

Business Expenses: rent, utilities, phone, mobile phones, Internet, salaries, gas, cleaners, stamps, envelopes, office chairs, furniture, uniforms, gloves, business cards, marketing materials, etc. *Everything* that your business relies on for a 30-day period needs to be documented. Do not leave anything out. Count all of your recurring costs. This is how you will determine if your business will fit and sustain in the marketplace. When you have completed your checklist, add the total cost of everything and then divide by 30 days. This answer will reveal how much you spend every day to stay in business.

Can your business sustain this cost? This is also a formula to determine the price of your product.

Some small businesses price their product based upon what a competitor may price their product. This is not sound judgment because you do not know what their costs are. Suppose a competitor's rent is $1,700 per month and yours is $400 per month. That is a $1,300 difference. That is a lot of money for a small business. That means that you have the opportunity to sell your product well below market prices. However, if you are not diligent in your monthly cost structure, you are missing the opportunity to capitalize on your competitor by 25 percent. That is a huge savings for you and a gigantic leap over your competitor. Profit margins are determined by your monthly fixed costs against your monthly sales. Keeping your fixed costs to a bare minimum will keep your profit margins in the black.

The Best Tax Structure for Your Business

Before we go into business and put our product into the marketplace, we want to find out what is the best way to structure our business from a liability standpoint and from a tax standpoint. Taxes are always the elephant in the room. We stay up late at night trying to figure out how we can keep more money in our pockets and give less to Uncle Sam. We understand that taxes are a major part of our economy, but we do not want to pay taxes on anything that is not generating a profit.

Most entrepreneurs align their business name with "Inc." at the end. What does that mean? Companies use these acronyms for a reason. It lets Uncle Sam (IRS) know if your business is a for-profit or nonprofit organization. This is important! You have to get a firm understanding of how you want to be recognized in the business community and to everyone else, including the IRS, customers, suppliers, lawyers and accountants. Whatever you choose will have an immediate impact on your personal and/or business life cycle.

So let us be clear, we are here to make money! When we get it, we do not want to lose it because we are positioned into a structure that is not beneficial to our business. Nor do we want to be in a position where our liability puts us at a disadvantage.

Below are some scenarios that you should consider when setting up your business entity:

SOLE PROPRIETORSHIP

Advantages

- Easy to form; not much start-up paperwork required.

- There is no one to split profits with.

- Decisions can be made quickly.

- No double taxation business gains or losses reported on individual tax returns (Schedule C).

- Losses offset income from other sources, jobs, interests, etc.

Disadvantages

- There is unlimited personal liability.

- Business may terminate with your disability or death.

- Do not qualify for some tax advantages that corporations receive, such as insurance, medical reimbursement, retaining earnings in business for expansion.

PARTNERSHIP

Advantages

- No formal agreement is required.

- No conflict of interest possible.

- Each partner has a fiduciary relationship to the other.

- Percentage owned by each does not have to be equal.

- More capital may be available.

Disadvantages

- Each partner acts as agent for all the others.

- Personal assets are in jeopardy.

- Partnership may dissolve upon death or withdrawal of any partner.

- May be difficult to get rid of an undesirable partner.

LIMITED PARTNERSHIP

(In Georgia, an agreement is required)

- Limited partner is more like a stockholder.

- Only liable up to the amount paid into the partnership.

- Do not participate in management.

- Can sell his/her interest without consent.

- Partnership can legally survive death or withdrawal.

What to Include in any Partnership Agreement

- Character of partners – general, limited, etc.

- Contributions by partners at inception, at later date

- Business expenses – how handled

- Authority – limits on agency

- Division of profits and losses

- Draws or salary

- Death of a partner

- Sale of partnership interest

- Settlements of disputes

- Absence and/or disability of a partner

Steps in Forming a Corporation in Georgia

1. Obtain a Name Registration Certificate from the Secretary of State.

2. If Secretary of State determines name is available, he or she will issue the certificate for $25.

3. File Articles of Incorporation with Secretary of State, $100.

4. Shareholders must contribute a minimum of $500.

5. Advertise in legal periodical of county; send check for $40 made out to the periodical with articles and letter asking

editor to publish notice of incorporation once per week for two weeks.

"S" CORPORATION

(Formerly Subchapter S)

- Enjoy immunity from unlimited personal liability and avoid double taxation.

- Must form during first two and a half months of the tax year in which it is to go into effect.

- File Form 2553 with the IRS – pay no corporate income taxes, file only an information return, and income and loss become part of personal tax return.

- Seventy-five or fewer shareholders; only individuals or stabs.

- Only one class of outstanding stock.

- All shareholders must consent.

- Portion of receipts must be derived from active business rather than passive investments.

- No limit on size of corporation's income and assets.

- In Georgia, stockholders who are non-residents of Georgia must file and pay taxes. Check the laws in your state.

Insurance

1. Find an agent.

2. Get references from other professionals.

3. Look for CLU or CP/CU designation.

4. Use an insurance consultant.

Licenses, Permits and Other Red Tape

- Employer's Identification Number (EIN) – SS-4 and CRF-002; must have these even if you have no employees.

- Business License, either city or county.

- Other requirements if your business involves a cable television franchise, massage pawnshops, poolrooms, beer and wine or liquor, peddling, home business, precious metals.

- State – Check with your State's Secretary of State Office.

- Federal – investment counseling, making alcohol or tobacco, meat, firearms, drugs, starting a radio or television station.

Food Sales Establishment License

- Food processing or grocery sales

- Inspection necessary

- Get copy of rules and regulations from the Department of
  Agriculture in your state.

Alcoholic Beverage License

- If you plan to sell beer, wine or more, be sure to check the
  laws in your state.

Taxes

Get from IRS:

- Mr. Businessman's Kit

- Tax Guide for Small Business

Examine a Building Lease for the Following Clauses

- Look for short-term or month-to-month

- What are the provisions for putting up a sign?

- Can you make improvements or alterations?

- Option to renew

- Right to sublet or assign

- Who does repairs, maintenance, and pays utilities, taxes and insurance?

Sales Contracts

- Obtain copies from competitors, trade associations, office supply
- Remember to require proof of customer's age to avoid contracting with minors.

Entrepreneurs Beware

It took me some time to figure out that all is fair when it comes to doing business in the United States. It does not matter if you are a start-up or seasoned business owner. If you expose a weak link, your competitor will seize the moment. Whenever an entrepreneur comes up with a bright idea, it is only natural for him or her to try to turn it into a business. It is the American way. There is also an industry out there that likes to take advantage of your excitement and enthusiasm. It is perfectly legal and it is profitable. I have known entrepreneurs that have paid up to $2,000 just to get a business license, business name, and EIN. I was blown away! I could not believe it. I paid less than $300 to get started, including my EIN.

In Georgia, we go to the Secretary of State website to get ourselves registered. This website is loaded with information pertaining to opening up a business where you live. It only costs you $100 to incorporate your business with the state; $25 to secure a business name; $40 to advertise in a legal periodical (local newspaper) and $108 for a business license (Cobb County). Setting up a business where you live is cheaper than you think.

Each state has its own set of rules when it comes to doing business in that state. You must abide by their business statute and laws, but they also have a Secretary of State website that will help you set up your business and stay in accordance with the law. They can explain to you the difference between S-Corporation, Sole Proprietorship, Limited Liability Corporation, Nonprofits or Partnership. EINs are free at the IRS.org website.

Do not let this venture scare you into thinking that you must have $2,000 to get yourself up and running. I strongly suggest that you do this on your own because it is so simple, and you could save hundreds of dollars in the process. Do not be one of those entrepreneurs who are too busy to save a buck. As an entrepreneur, we have to keep a keen eye on the bottom line. Just as we are excited to get up and running, there are those who are anxious to see us coming.

To get the benefits of owning a business you have to start with an EIN. You can get an EIN at IRS.org. There you will also find critical information that is directly related to your business from a tax perspective. Consult your tax advisor for more specific information.

If you are doing business on the Internet, you will want to establish a .COM name so that customers may find you. These are some of the leading domain name providers in the industry: NetworkSolutions.com., Go Daddy.com and Name.com. The service is the same but the pricing is different. Here you can search to see………….. Choose what is best for you and your budget.

"Success is really about being ready for opportunity; you can't plan innovation or inspiration, but you can be ready for it."

—Eric Schmidt

MENTORSHIP

I have come to learn that the word mentorship carries a lot of weight. By definition, it refers to a *personal developmental relationship* in which a more experienced or more knowledgeable person helps a less experienced or less knowledgeable person. A mentor is one of the most valuable resources that you can have. It must be someone that is above your status, someone that you respect and trust, and someone who you can communicate with that does not intimidate you. You develop a bond with that person, a businesslike kinship. It is a great position to be in because mentors can share information that can turn your whole program around. Pay close attention to them because what they say is important and they like speaking to someone who is actually listening to them. You become sort of a personal protégé. They will spend time with you to make sure you succeed.

Most of us concentrate on the business that we are trying to get off the ground, not realizing how much information already lays in our spirit. Sometimes a mentor can bring things out of you that you did not know you had in you. What you think is worthless could be more valuable than you comprehend. That is how I am with you today. Out of all the ideas I have come up with in the past, writing an entrepreneur guide to success was not one of them. In fact, some of my close associates will be very surprised when this hits the market. Please understand that I put myself in this position. I believe that when preparation meets opportunity, success is sure to follow.

"Business owners value the process of entrepreneurship , customers value the Results!"

                                                    -Mack Arthur Parks Jr

Never Throw Away Your Rough Drafts

This chapter of the book was not in my original plans. It became necessary as I began to write. I came to the conclusion that entrepreneurs should *never* throw away their drafts. They are a valuable asset to your mindset and your business going forward. Unbelievably, people will actually pay for a lot of the information that you have gathered. You may not realize it, but it took a lot of time, energy and effort for you to pull that information from the deepest corners of your mind and bring it to the forefront. I envision you using a ladder to climb down a dark space in your mind that you have not seen in awhile. Once you get down there, you turn the light on and start looking around. You start seeing things that have value that you forgot about. Moreover, while you were down there looking for answers to your current project, you found answers to questions that you had not even thought of. I am sure you ran across something else that you could use later down the line, like metaphors or slogans. You cannot afford to let this slip away. *Write it down*! When your mind is activated like this, it goes in automatic mode. You start thinking about things you did not plan on; actually, you find yourself sitting and thinking and then all of a sudden good things just start coming to you. It is like magic. You will find yourself on a roll. Words and phrases start coming out of you so fast that you will have to write it down quickly before you forget what you are thinking.

When you are finished rolling through your mind, you have to climb back up the ladder and turn the light off. Once you turn that light off, that's it! If you did not write it down, it is gone. Seize the moments you have by writing your thoughts on paper. You may not use it right away, but it can be useful to you down the line.

Do you remember the thought process that it took you to think of a company name? Was that easy? What about that letter you wrote to a potential client a few months ago? Can you recite what it said? What about the letters you wrote to your suppliers, banker, customers or the Small Business Administration (SBA)? Do you remember what you asked or said in those letters? What about all the telephone numbers and contacts you made, their names and titles? You cannot just make this stuff up. It took some work! People are always moving on, but the contact information remains the same. This is very good work that you have done.

When I was putting the story together for this book, I had to rely on information that I gathered nearly 15 years ago. I could not remember whom I spoke to off the top of my head, so I had to look at some of my drafts and read what I said and to whom I sent it. That information was rewarding because the person that I spoke to is no longer there, but I know exactly what I talked about and the contact information is still the same. I am so happy that I had the insight to

keep all of my drafts. I hope your drafts will reward you as well.

To all Department Heads: We must maximize our efforts in order to

stretch every dollar we can.

Every penny counts! Keep an eye on your *money*!

Despite what people say about the economy, the world *is turning green.*

What you write has value; it is a resource that you will soon cherish. Never throw away your drafts!

I want to thank you for taking the time to read my book, and I hope I shared some valuable insight and knowledge with you in order to get your business up and running. When I write the next book on this subject, I will talk about pricing, projections, forecasting, cost analysis, start-up costs, ROI (Return on Investment), Executive Summary and Funding.

Now is the time to gather your thoughts on what you just read and start writing down all the wonderful ideas you have been thinking about. Please remember to attempt one business idea at a time because researching your competitors and industry takes up a lot of valuable time. *Use all of your energy on what is going to make you successful.*

www.ingramcontent.com/pod-product-compliance
Lightning Source LLC
Chambersburg PA
CBHW060614210326
41520CB00010B/1327